CONTENTS

Frontispiece:
EDWARD SEYMOUR, 1st Duke of Somerset
*Reproduced by kind permission of the Marquis of Bath
Longleat House, Warminster, Wiltshire*

ACKNOWLEDGEMENTS

I am grateful to George Bernard, Barbara Harvey and Paul Slack for reading this piece, and for much other help. I have also gained from discussions with John King, perhaps the more so since we disagree so profoundly about Somerset. All my Special Subject pupils have, over the years, contributed in some way.

**Protector Somerset
a reassessment**

by

Jennifer Loach

HEADSTART HISTORY

Published by   HEADSTART HISTORY
                PO Box 41, Bangor, Gwynedd, LL57 1SB

Typeset by   CELTIC TYPESETTERS & PRINTERS
                Rainbow Business Centre
                Swansea Enterprise Park
                Llansamlet, Swansea SA7 9EH

Printed by   The Book Factory, London

ISBN   1 873041 50 0

A CIP catalogue record for this book is available from the British Library.

I — A ROYAL MARRIAGE

Early in 1536 Henry VIII, tiring of his second wife, Anne Boleyn, fell in love with one of her ladies-in-waiting, Jane Seymour. Precisely when Jane's quiet charms first attracted the king's attention is unclear; her father, a substantial Wiltshire gentleman, Sir John Seymour of Wulf Hall, had entertained both Henry and Anne in his home for a week in early September 1535, but there is no evidence that Jane was present on that occasion, and some historians have suggested that the love affair did not begin until Jane's elder brother, Edward, was appointed a gentleman of Henry's privy chamber in March 1536, for in that position of influence close to the king he may have served, as Professor Ives has somewhat unkindly put it, as 'his sister's ponce'.[1]

On 30 May 1536, only eleven days after Anne Boleyn had been executed for adultery and treason, Henry and Jane Seymour were married. Jane's elevation brought considerable benefits to Sir John's numerous family. A week after the ceremony her eldest brother was created viscount Beauchamp, and in August he became Chancellor and Chamberlain of North Wales; by March 1537 he was a member of the privy council.[2] He was also given a substantial grant of land from dissolved, or about-to-be dissolved, monasteries. Another of the new queen's brothers, Thomas, became a gentleman of the privy chamber, and steward of manors in Wales and the Marches, whilst a third, Henry, was appointed steward of a number of royal manors. In October 1537 Jane did what none of Henry's other wives were to do: she produced a healthy male child. In acknowledgement, Henry raised his eldest brother-in-law to the earldom of Hertford, and knighted Thomas. But a week after the baby's splendid christening, at which Hertford carried the young Princess Elizabeth, Jane Seymour died.

---

1 E. W. Ives, *Anne Boleyn* (Oxford, 1986), 247.
2 J. Guy, *Tudor England* (Oxford, 1988), 161.

This could have been the end of her brothers' advancement: Henry certainly slipped after her death into honourable obscurity. But Edward and Thomas were made of sterner stuff. Thomas prospered, going on embassies to Vienna and the Netherlands, and receiving a number of important military commissions. Edward did even better. He remained a royal intimate; at an audience in January 1538, for example, the king 'stood leaning against the cupboard', with Cromwell and Hertford at his side, and later the same year, when Henry gave a banquet for a few special guests, Hertford and his wife were included.[3]

By the early 1540s Hertford had considerable political and military experience. In addition to service on the council and on the battlefield, he had gone on a number of diplomatic missions, including one to the emperor, Charles V. He was also by that time a man of considerable wealth.[4] In 1537 he recorded that Henry VIII had bestowed on him lands worth over six hundred pounds a year: more was to come, and by Henry's death Hertford had an annual income from land of over eleven hundred pounds.[5]

II — HENRY VIII'S LAST MONTHS

Hertford was thus in a strong position when, in the summer of 1546, war with France came to an end. The court filled up with strong and ambitious men, whose competitiveness increased as the ageing king grew more feeble. Amongst those jockeying for supreme authority, informed observers picked out two — John Dudley, viscount Lisle, and Hertford; in December 1546, when it had become clear that the king was seriously ill, the imperial ambassador even reported a rumour that, on his death, custody of the Prince and the government of the realm would be entrusted to Hertford and Dudley.

3 M. St. Clare Byrne (ed.), *Lisle Letters* (6 vols., Chicago), V, 10, 285-6.

4 J. E. Jackson, 'Wulfhall and the Seymours', *Wiltshire Archaeological Magazine*, xv, 189.

5 H. Miller, *Henry VIII and the English Nobility* (Oxford, 1986), 235.

The rise of Lisle and Hertford was facilitated by certain changes in the structure of the court which took place at this time — indeed, so helpful to them were these changes that it has been suggested that there existed a wide-ranging plot master-minded by Listle and Hertford, a plot intended to put the religious radicals into a dominant position.[6] Firstly, there was a significant transformation in the personnel of the privy chamber, that is, amongst the men who helped the king to wash and dress, to eat and sleep, and to fill his idle moments: in October 1546, three months before Henry's death, one of the two chief gentlemen of the privy chamber, Thomas Heneage, was abruptly dismissed, to be replaced by Sir William Herbert.[7] Heneage was a religious conservative, whilst Herbert, the brother-in-law of Henry's last wife, Katherine Parr, was, it is argued, a radical. Secondly, Stephen Gardiner, bishop of Winchester, quarrelled with the king, and was therefore excluded from the council set up by Henry to run the country during Edward's minority. Thirdly, the earl of Surrey and his father, the duke of Norfolk, were convicted of treason. Surrey was executed, his father saved by Henry's own death. Both were attainted, however, and consequently all the considerable Howard land-holding thereby came into the king's hands. It was a hoard upon which many greedy eyes were fixed.

However, there is no need to attribute any of these events to a radical plot. Herbert's supposed radical religious leanings turn out, when carefully examined, to consist largely of guilt by association, as the husband of a woman praised by the humanist Ascham, and as the brother-in-law of a queen sometimes described as the furtherer of protestantism. But Herbert was also the grandson of an earlier earl of Pembroke, and had been in royal service since the middle of the 1520s: his claims to advancement were genuine, although they were doubtless increased by his relationship

6 D. Starkey, *The Reign of Henry VIII: Personalities and Politics* (London, 1985), chapter 7.
7 Starkey, *Henry VIII*, 156-7.

to the queen. His claims to be a religious radical were, however, slight; in 1550 the imperial ambassador even declared that Herbert 'knows no other language but his native English, and can neither read nor write'.

What of Gardiner's fall from favour? This can be more plausibly explained, as Glyn Redworth has suggested, by Gardiner's own stubbornness and miscalculations than by the deliberate machinations of his religious opponents.[8] Henry was personally and fixedly hostile to Gardiner throughout at least the second half of 1546; Foxe tells us that even before his last illness the king would not grant Gardiner an audience when he appeared with the other councillors.[9] When, in December 1546, Henry decided to change the list of executors named in the will that he had written at the time of the Boulogne expedition of 1544 so as to exclude Gardiner, and one of the gentlemen of the chamber, Sir Anthony Browne, remonstrated with him, Henry was firm. He said that the bishop was a 'troublesome' man who would seek to overawe the other executors; he himself 'could use him and rule him', but others would not be able to do so.[10]

Equally, there is no need of a conspiracy theory to explain the fall of the house of Howard. Surrey had, without doubt, behaved in a reckless and autocratic way. Investigations revealed that he had quartered his arms with those of Edward the Confessor, the most revered of English kings, thereby making a claim to royal blood which Henry could hardly ignore; he had also made some wild assertions about aristocratic privilege, and uttered threats against various members of the council, including Hertford, who were, he claimed, of ignoble birth. Surrey was surely responsible for his own fate.

8 G. Redworth, *In Defence of the Church Catholic. The Life of Stephen Gardiner* (Oxford, 1990), 239-47.

9 Foxe, J., *Acts and Monuments*, ed. S. R. Cattley, 8 vols. (London, 1837), v, 691-2.

10 For a full account, see E. W. Ives, 'Henry VIII's Will: A Forensic Conundrum', *Historical Journal*, 35 (1992), 779-804.

4

Thus, although the fall of the Howards, and the disgrace of Gardiner may have been part of a carefully orchestrated plot, the balance of the evidence suggests that they were not. If there was no plot, there is no need to attribute responsibility to Hertford and Lisle. But if we dismiss the notion of a conspiracy in the last months of Henry's life we are left with the problem of Henry's apparently surprising choice of executors for his will. The 1536 Succession Act had empowered the king, by his will, to appoint guardians for a minor heir, and Henry accordingly named sixteen executors who were to have 'the Government' of his son and his realms until the nine-year-old Edward reached the age of eighteen.[11] It has been argued that the executors named in the extant will present a less balanced and uncommitted aspect than might have been expected of a body nominated by the cautious and conservative Henry, and that Lisle and Hertford were again responsible for considerable behind-the-scenes meddling. But if the list is carefully examined, the evidence for a radical bias is by no means conclusive. Archbishop Cranmer was, obviously, of a reforming disposition, but he was balanced by the much more traditionalist Tunstal, bishop of Durham, who was to be deprived later in Edward's reign. William, Lord St. John [Paulet] was notorious for his willingness to bend with the wind, and a number of the other executors should, like William Paget, be described as 'neuters'. The list does not seem fundamentally out of character with Henry's known religious inclinations, or, perhaps more important, with his judgement on the administrative and political skills of those who served him. To suggest that Henry was fully responsible for the list of executors is not, of course, to deny that the will poses a number of problems; indeed, the very validity of the document was later questioned, since Henry did not sign it with his own hand, as the 1536 act required, but apparently sanctioned instead the use of the dry stamp, a means of securing

11 D. Hoak, *The King's Council in the Reign of Edward VI* (Cambridge, 1976), 34-46.

a facsimile of the king's signature by inking-in an impression produced by a seal.[12] But Professor Ives has recently made light of these problems, arguing that the will did indeed 'spell out the king's intentions . . . for the government of the country during the minority of his son'.[13] The issue remains open.

III — THE ESTABLISHMENT OF THE PROTECTORSHIP

In any case, the will was of short-lived effect, for only three days after Henry's death, on 31 January 1547, the executors elected one of their number, Hertford, as protector of the realm. This change was formalised on 4 February when the young king and thirteen of the executors of Henry's will signed a commission giving sovereign authority to Hertford until Edward reached the age of eighteen, and by letters-patent granted on 12 March. On 1 March a new council of twenty-six members was established: however, a few days later one of those councillors, the chancellor, Thomas Wriothesley, newly-created earl of Southampton, was struck off. The reason given publicly for his dismissal was a complaint laid against him by some common lawyers, but a number of contemporary sources claimed that the real reason why he lost office was because he was 'sore against' the establishment of the protectorate; as Dale Hoak puts it, Southampton was forced out not because 'the common lawyers may have opposed his practices, but because (he) had from the very beginning opposed [Hertford's] creation as Protector'.[14]

The exact process by which Edward Seymour came to be chosen as protector is difficult to discern, for statements

12 Starkey, *Henry VIII*, 136.

13 Ives, 'Henry VIII's Will: A Forensic Conundrum', *804.

14 He suggests that Southampton may have refused to affix the great seal to letters confirming Somerset's elevation (Hoak, *King's Council*, 43, 235-7).

made later, at the time of his fall, have to be treated with some scepticism. But three things are certain. The first is that William Paget acted, in a sense, as Hertford's agent; later he was to remind the Protector of what he had promised him in the gallery at Westminster 'before his breath was out' of Henry's body.[15] Secondly, although the executors were undoubtedly within their rights in choosing to hand over power to the young king's uncle — Henry's will had provided that a majority of them could 'devise and ordain' whatever they thought best for the government of the king and of the realm — there can be little doubt that their willingness to do so was encouraged by a promise of a substantial distribution of titles and lands.

A few days after the decision to make Hertford Protector had been taken Paget, Denny and Herbert formally recorded for the council what they 'remembered' of things that Henry had intended to put into his will, but had somehow forgotten to do. These memories resulted in the elevation of Hertford to the dukedom of Somerset, of William Parr to the marquisate of Northampton, of Lisle to the earldom of Warwick, and of Thomas Wriothesley to the earldom of Southampton. Four new barons were created, and crown land worth well over £3000 a year, most of it previously belonging to the Howards, was distributed. ALmost all the executors received hand-outs.[16]

Amongst those who did well from what has been called Henry VIII's 'unwritten will' was the Protector's younger brother, Sir Thomas Seymour. He received land worth £500 p.a., and, although he had been named by Henry only as one of the 'assistant' executors,[17] he also, at the very beginning of February 1547, became a privy councillor. He was soon after appointed Lord Admiral. Thus, the third point

15 J. Strype, *Ecclesiastical Memorials; relating chiefly to Religion and the Reformation* (London, 1816), VI, 421.

16 H. Miller, 'Henry VIII's Unwritten Will: grants of lands and honours in 1547', in E. W. Ives, R. J. Ives and J. J. Scarisbrick, eds., *Wealth and Power in Tudor England: essays presented to S. T. Bindoff* (London, 1978), 87-106.

17 Hoak, *King's Council*, 232-3.

that is certain about the process by which Edward Seymour became Protector is that his younger brother was far from happy about events, and needed to be bought off. Some accounts suggest that John Dudley, already plotting to seize power from his rival, encouraged Thomas Seymour in his anger against his elder brother. This may be so, but, as we shall see, Seymour's subsequent behaviour also suggests that he was a vain and impetuous man who would readily feel aggrieved without the need for intervention by a third party.[18]

But the probability that a certain amount of plotting and bribery surrounded Hertford's elevation should not obscure the fact that the elevation was a sensible and entirely traditional move. Sixteenth-century government was only with difficulty run by committees, and the conduct of warfare, in particular, was extremely cumbersome without a sole directing hand. A regency, in some shape or form, was a well-established solution to the accession of a minor. The obvious person to be regent was the monarch's mother or his paternal uncle. But Edward's mother had died giving birth to him, and he had no paternal uncles. The choice therefore, logically enough, fell upon his maternal uncle. Indeed, Henry may have had some such idea in his mind: according to an account given by one of Henry's secretaries, William Clerk, when Henry was too ill to sign his will, it was to Hertford that he gave the document in a token of assent and in the presence of witnesses.

IV — SOMERSET'S PERSONALITY

What was he like, the new Protector? Few sixteenth-century politicians have received more favourable treatment from twentieth-century historians than Somerset. From the publication in 1900 of A. F. Pollard's *England under Protector Somerset* he has been portrayed by

---

18 See page 21.

most English and American scholars as an idealist, concerned primarily with reform of church and state: indeed, some have created a liberal dreamer who would not have felt out of place at early meetings of the Fabian Society.[19] 'Ambitious he certainly was', wrote Pollard, 'yet his was an ambition animated by no mean or selfish motives, but by the desire to achieve aims that were essentially noble'; the Protector, 'ardent and enthusiastic by nature', fixed his gaze on a distant goal 'and overlooked the obstacles that beset his feet'.[20] W. K. Jordan followed Pollard in his admiration: his verdict of Somerset is that he was a 'very great man whose magnanimity and high idealism were never to be forgotten as Englishmen spoke in quiet corners, in the fields and on the sea of the age of the "Good Duke" '.[21] Such views ill-accord with the man of action that Somerset primarily was. Knighted in the field by the duke of Suffolk on the French expedition of 1523, he had served in both Scotland and France in the last years of Henry's reign; he had been appointed, briefly, warden of the Scottish marches, was responsible in 1544 for the sacking of Edinburgh Castle, and the next year for a spectacular defence of Boulogne against the French. His actions as Protector were to demonstrate his interest in military matters; many of the earliest official letters of the protectorship, for example, concern the south coast defences, on which, between March and August 1547, £6000 was spent. (Another £4800 was paid out in the following year).[22] And, as we shall see, Somerset was preoccupied — M. L. Bush would say, obsessed — throughout the Protectorship with the problem of Scotland, the strengthening of the fortifications of the north being another of his early concerns.

19 The exception to this is, of course, M. L. Bush's magisterial study of *The Government Policy of Protector Somerset* (London, 1975). Bush's suggestion that Somerset was preoccupied with Scotland has been widely accepted, but the book has had surprisingly little impact on the general reputation of 'the good duke'.

20 A. F. Pollard, *Protector Somerset* (London, 1900), 317.

21 W. K. Jordan, *Edward VI: the Young King* (London, 1968), 523.

22 ed. H. M. Colvin, *The History of the King's Works*, IV (1485-1660), II (1982), 502-13.

Somerset was, then, as concerned about matters military as Henry had been. Moreover, and in this Somerset was unlike his former master, his interests were, in the main, confined to those of a soldier. Amongst the extant– and voluminous– accounts of Somerset's expenditure over the years there is little to suggest intellectual pursuits, although large sums were spent on jewellery and plate, and on building. (Somerset was also an inveterate gambler — winning, in 1542, thirty-five shillings 'the night he supped at Lambeth' with the archbishop of Canterbury.) However, it would be unfair to deduce from the accounts alone that Somerset owned no books, for we know that, in fact, he owned two; both were entirely appropriate fare for a military man, one being a French translation of a racy tale, Boccaccio's *Decameron*,[23] and the other a manuscript volume of tide tables.[24] He also maintained a troup of players.[25]

Nonetheless, Somerset's admirers have often claimed that he had a considerable interest in education; after all, an Elizabethan source credits the Protector with the view that

> if learning decay, which of wild men
> maketh civil, of blockish and rash persons
> wise and godly counsellors, and of evil men
> good and godly Christians; what shall we
> look for else but barbarism and tumult? [26]

One of the stated purposes of the dissolution of the chantries was to be the 'erecting of grammar schools to the education of youth in virtue and godliness, the further augmenting of the universities, and better provision of the poor and needy', but in the event most of the money went directly into the coffers of the crown; only those lands that

---

23 J. N. King, *English Reformation Literature. The Tudor Origins of the Protestant Tradition* (Princeton, 1982), 109.

24 It was, poignantly, into these that he wrote some verse on the eve of his death. See page 51.

25 S. R. Westfall, *Patrons and Performance. Early Tudor Household Revels* (Oxford, 1990), paasim.

26 W. Harrison, quoted by W. K. Jordan, in *Edward VI: the Young King* (London, 1968), 327. For a further discussion of this quotation, see G. T. R. Parry, 'Inventing the Good Duke of Somerset', *Journal of Ecclesiastical History* (40) 1989, 370-80.

were already used for the maintenance of schools appear to have been preserved.[27] One of those close to Somerset, John Hales, had founded a school in Coventry at the end of Henry's reign, but in general Somerset and his circle are not distinguished for their interest in schools.

There is, however, more evidence for an interest in university matters amongst those close to Somerset, and in 1548 the government ordered a visitation of Oxford and Cambridge.[28] One aim of the visitation was to remove all traces of popery from the universities, but it was also intended to produce a syllabus that was more practical, more 'relevant' to the needs of the day. A major proposal, which was much desired by the secretary to the council, Sir Thomas Smith, was, therefore, to amalgamate, in Cambridge, the colleges of Clare and Trinity Hall, and in Oxford, parts of New and All Souls, to produce establishments committed to the study of civil law.[29] This suggestion offended not only the fellows of the institutions concerned, who took prompt, and effective, action to protect themselves, but also alienated those who felt, like the reformer, Ridley, one of the commissioners for Cambridge, that it was 'a very sore thing, a great scandal . . . to take a college founded for the study of God's word, and to apply it to the use of students in man's law'. To this, Somerset replied pragmatically, pointing out how great was the need for civilians to assist the government in its interpretation of treaties.[30]

There is, then, very little evidence to support the view that Somerset was particularly committed to the advancement of education. The same is true of things spiritual. W. K. Jordan declared that 'Somerset was an undoubted

27 A. Kreider, *English Chantries: the Road to Dissolution* (Cambridge, Mass., 1979), 106-8.

28 C. Cross, 'Oxford and the Tudor State, 1509-1558', in J. McConica, ed. *The History of the University of Oxford*, III (Oxford, 1986), 135-8.

29 M. Dewar, *Sir Thomas Smith. A Tudor Intellectual in Office* (London, 1964), 40-2; Bush, *Government Policy*, 54-5.

30 Somerset made similar points in a letter to Gardiner: *The Letters of Stephen Gardiner*, ed. J. A. Muller (Cambridge, 1933), 493-5.

Protestant of moderate and Erastian persuasion',[31] but the evidence for any personal piety beyond the conventional is tenuous. Somerset had, of course, considerable religious patronage, and in Edward's reign he appointed a number of protestants to positions within his household, including his physician, William Turner,[32] and Thomas Becon, his chaplain.[33] He was also associated with Coverdale, who had served as almoner to the duke's one-time sister-in-law, Katherine Parr; in 1550 Somerset issued a commendatory dedication to a translation of Otto Werdmueller's *A spyrytuall and moost precyouse pearle* that was probably by Coverdale.[34] Because of the political troubles of the time John Hooper stayed with the Protector briefly after his return from exile in 1549, and, according to one of the foreign émigrés, it was Somerset who was responsible for his later elevation to the see of Gloucester.[35] But in the circumstances of the late 1540s these associations are no more than what one would expect of a man in Somerset's position; indeed, we might also observe that the duke was not, in general, conspicuous for his advancement of protestant clients.[36]

However, Somerset's duchess can be much more positively linked with reformers. Anne Stanhope, whom Somerset married as his second wife sometime before March 1535, was in 1546 involved with the radical Anne Askew, who was subsequently burnt for heresy; she was said to have sent a man in a blue coat with ten shillings to help her.[37] It was more probably through the influence of

31 *The Young King*, 125.
32 W. R. D. Jones, *William Turner. Tudor Naturalist, Physician and Divine* (London, 1988), 19-26. There is, however, *pace*, Bush (*Government Policy*, 108) no reason to believe that Somerset 'summoned' him from exile.
33 D. S. Bailey, *Thomas Becon and the Reformation of the Church in England* (Edinburgh, 1952), 54.
34 See page 14.
35 *Original Letters Relative to the English Reformation*, ed. H. Robinson (Parker Society, 1946-7), 68-9, 410.
36 See, for example, Bush, *Government Policy*, 111 and Jones, *William Turner*, 21, 23.
37 Foxe, *Acts and Monuments*, v, 547.

Anne Stanhope than that of her husband that their six daughters received a scholarly education; Becon, dedicating a revised edition of his *The gouernans of vertue* in 1550 to Lady Jane Seymour, praised her parents for bringing up both sons and daughers in 'good literature and in the knowledge of God's most holy laws'. By 1549 the duchess was widely recognised as a woman of radical religious views, and the eminent academic and civil servant, Thomas Smith, found it necessary to justify himself to her in very defensive terms, saying that he was no religious neuter, but a man who had 'professed Christ' in the 'times of persecution'.

But if Somerset left most matters intellectual and spiritual to his wife, why was he the recipient of no less than twenty-four book and manuscript dedications?[38] (His wife received the dedication of eleven religious works between Edward's accession and October 1551.[39]) After all, even the king himself received only forty-nine, and Warwick a mere seven.

Some of the dedications came from Somerset's clients. William Turner dedicated to him *The names of herbes in Greke, Latin, Englishe . . .* and *A new herball*, and William Gray, one of his household, gave him gifts of verse. But a dedication did not necessarily indicate that a relationship existed between the author and the dedicatee; thus, William Gibson, a school-master at Sherborne, was probably unknown to Somerset until he sent him a translation of one of Bullinger's works.

Only two of these works deserve specific attention. In April 1550 there appeared *An Epistle of Godly Consolacion . . .*, a letter of Calvin's written during the rebellions of the previous year. The frontispiece claims that the work was 'trans-

38 F. Williams, *An Index of Dedications and Commendatory Verse in English Books before 1642* (London), 1962); J. N. King, 'Protector Somerset, Patron of the English Renassiance', *Papers of the Bibliographical Society of America*, 70 (1976), 326-31, and *English Reformation Literature*, 107-8, 460-1.

39 I am grateful to Dakota L. Hamilton for these figures.

lated out of frenshe' by the duke, but the preface, which probably was indeed written by Somerset, in no way supports this. However, the preface itself is of some interest, for it rejoices in the coming-forth of 'godly preachers' who spoke out against the sin of rebellion, and in the fact that 'little England' was now successfully resisting foreign power. The second work which sheds some light on Somerset himself is a translation of Otto Werdmueller's *A Spyrytuall and Moost Precyouse Pearle,* which appeared the following month. This, again, has a commendatory preface by Somerset, in which he says that Werdmueller's book had given him consolation in his 'great trouble', and that he had therefore asked 'him of whom we had the copy' — who was, in fact, Miles Coverdale — to ensure its setting-forth, in order that others might find in the book the consolation in affliction that he had.[40]

Does all this justify a description of Somerset as 'a Protestant patron and man of letters'? Book dedications are not, in truth, a very helpful guide to the religious views of the dedicatee. In 1548 William Forrest dedicated to Somerset his 'Pleasaunt Poesy of Princelie Practise', presumably because it dealt with matters agrarian, and he also dedicated to him his translation of the psalms. But Forrest was a conservative priest, who later became a chaplain to Queen Mary, and his best known work is a history of the patient and badly-treated 'Griseld', Catherine of Aragon; he made a strange bed-fellow for Turner and Coverdale. Henry Parker, Lord Morley, who dedicated to Somerset a manuscript commentary on Ecclesiastes, was a member of the household of the Princess Mary, to whom he dedicated a number of other works; interestingly, Morley threw in his lot with Somerset's opponents very early in the coup of 1549. Lord Stafford, another conservative, was responsible for the dedication to the Protector of a translation of *de vera differentia,* a work by

---

40 Jordan, *The Young King,* 126, implies that Somerset declared that Werdmueller's book had consoled him after his fall: in fact, Somerset says that it had been a comfort during the previous year's popular risings.

the Henrician bishop, Edward Fox, which would certainly have been disapproved of by the radicals.

Any person in a position of power in the sixteenth century was likely to receive dedications from authors anxious to find patronage, for dedications were both a form of courtesy and a request for patronage. It is note-worthy that Somerset received no dedications before he became Protector, and that his wife received none between his fall and the middle of Elizabeth's reign; it was their position rather than their beliefs that had brought them so many dedications.

Nonetheless, Warwick's supreme authority did not, as we have seen, produce the same result. Does this suggest that intellectuals and men of religion saw him in a different light from that in which they had regarded Somerset? The range of subjects amongst the books dedicated to Warwick is not unlike those addressed to the Protector, some being religious — John Bale's *An expostulation . . . agaynste the blasphemyes of a franticke papyst . . .*, for example — and there were also works on rhetoric and geography. A significant fact here is the total number of books being published: from the peaks of 1548 and 1550 when over two hundred and fifty books were produced in a year, the average production slumped to about one hundred and fifty in the early 1550s, not rising again to over two hundred until 1555.[41] Although the change was in part due to the disastrous economic circumstances of the early 1550s, it is probably also true that the liberalisation of the treason and heresy laws at the beginning of Edward's reign, and a changed religious climate, produced in the late 1540s a particularly favourable environment for publishing, and for this Somerset should be given credit.[42]

41 for a discussion of book production see J. Loach, 'The Marian Establishment and the Printing Press', *English Historical Review*, 101 (1986), 136-7. The figures used here, however, are taken from a 1990 survey by the Institute of Bibliography of the University of Leeds.

42 It should, however, be noted that the government was not responsible for the bulk of the bill's more moderate provisos, which were added by the House of Commons (Bush, *Government Policy*, 145).

The changes in the treason and heresy laws that brought about this period of press freedom also, of course, permitted considerable religious discussion, and a number of people are known to have expressed openly opinions for which they would earlier have been burnt. No one was, in fact, burnt during the Protectorate: a remarkable record for the sixteenth century. Somerset must, obviously, take some credit for this; perhaps, as Jordan suggests, he did not believe that 'force was a proper or a useful instrument in religious policy'.[43] Certainly he was reported by Gardiner as having declared, pragmatically, that he 'would condemn other countries' that had different religious policies. But the bulk of the praise for this toleration should go to Cranmer, who carried out some very delicate interrogations with tact and sympathy; even in the much more difficult conditions that prevailed after the 1549 risings, only two people were burnt.

In any case, the liberal atmosphere of the early Protectorate soon changed. From May 1548 preaching was strictly regulated, and in September of that year it was totally forbidden. Moreover, in April 1549 a commission against heresy was issued, nominating twenty-five people, of whom two thirds were clergy; a number of people were summoned before it, but the majority abjured.

What little direct evidence there is for Somerset's religious views in the late 1540s suggests a man of some piety but little specialised knowledge, whose inclinations were, perhaps as a result of his wife's influence, towards the radical rather than the conservative end of the spectrum.[44] He was thought to have abandoned mass in his own household by December 1547 — but the same was claimed of Warwick and of Katherine Parr. (Nonetheless, the use of English in

43 Jordan, *The Young King*, 126-7. For a most interesting discussion of Somerset's toleration, or lack of it, see Bush, *Government Policy*, 112-9.

44 For a much more positive account of Somerset's religious views, see John King, 'Freedom of the Press, Protestant Propganda, and Protector Somerset', *Huntington Library Quarterly*, XL, (1976), 1-9; 'Protector Somerset, Patron of the English Renaissance', *Papers of the Bibliographical Society of America*, 70 (1976), 307-31; and *English Reformation Literature*, passim.

the Chapel Royal in April 1547, and for parts of the mass for the opening of parliament in the following November cannot have occurred without the Protector's specific sanction.) Somerset was not personally generous to the many distinguished protestant scholars who flocked to England to escape the persecution of the Emperor Charles V — they depended on the charity of Cranmer and of the young king — but he did not help the refugee protestant community at Glastonbury; however, there his charitable instincts ran alongside a hope that the Walloon weavers might prove a sound investment. (In the event, neither side fulfilled its part of the contract.)

Much of the religious change of this period, change that was sanctioned by the Protector even if it was not initiated by him, should be seen primarily as an attempt to consolidate the royal supremacy and to extend lay control over the church rather than as an effort to move the church in a specifically protestant direction. Thus, the Visitation of 1547 suspended the power of the bishops and other ordinaries, replacing it by that of thirty Visitors, of whom twenty were laymen. Moreover, by an act of 1547 'for the election of bishops' the old system whereby the dean and chapter were issued with a *congé d'elire*, or licence to elect, was abolished, and replaced by letters patent issuing directly from the monarch. Most important of all, the Prayer Book of 1549 was sanctioned merely by parliament, and not by the clerical gathering of convocation.

Other statutes of the period, such as the 1547 act for the giving of chantries and colleges to the king, were clearly intended primarily to provide the crown with much-needed funds; in a minute of the following year ordering the sale of some chantry land, the privy council stated that the dissolution was intended primarily to relieve the king's 'charges and expenses, which do daily grow and increase'.[45] Many dioceses were raided during the Protectorate: Lincoln lost

45 Kreider, *English Chantries*, 262.

thirty manors, Bath and Wells twenty, Norwich twelve and Exeter nine.[46] (Indeed, Felicity Heal has characterised Somerset's attitude towards the church as 'essentially acquisitive', noting that even when his main purpose was to secure additional funds for the crown 'the choice of dioceses to be assailed seems to have been determined largely by his own personal concerns'.[47] All clerics must have held their breath when the council ordered inventories of church plate to be made on a diocesan basis in December 1547, and then, in February 1549, asked for them to be done county by county: in the event, it was not until 1553 that the churches were actually stripped.[48] Thus, whilst the attack on the church's wealth was not as fierce in the Protectorate as it was subsequently to become, and Somerset seems to have been more sympathetic to the bishops than Warwick was to be, relations between church and state were throughout Edward's reign very much what might have been expected under a son of Henry VIII.

Altogether, therefore, the real Somerset was very different from the character whom historians have created in their own image. He was, for example, neither a modest nor a self-effacing man. From the beginning of his Protectorship, he conducted himself with great state; the imperial ambassador reported on 10 February 1547 that Somerset had two gilt maces borne before him, and he even took the royal jewels from Catherine Parr and allowed his wife to wear them.[49] He was extremely interested in money, a fact admitted even by Pollard, and in his pursuit of material advantage he could be both ruthless and cold-hearted.[50] Indeed,

---

46 F. Heal, *Of Prelates and Princes. A Study of the economic and Social Position of the Tudor Episcopate* (Cambridge, 1980), 131.

47 Ibid, 137.

48 C. E. Challis, *The Tudor Coinage* (Manchester, 1978), 163-4.

49 He may have gone further. One of the charges against him was the 'he hath robbed and embezzled from the king's majesty's the treasure and Jewels left by his majesty's father'.

50 See, for example, M. L. Bush, 'The Lisle-Seymour Land Disputes; a study of power and influence in the s', *Historical Journal*, I (1966), 255-64; Miller, *Henry VIII and the English Nobility*, 28-9, 252-3.

van der Delft reported that everyone found Somerset a 'dry, sour and opinionated man'. He was no twentieth century 'liberal', for a study by R. W. Heinze of his use of proclamations — proclamations are royal mandates, sealed with the great seal, and publicly proclaimed — revealed both that Somerset used proclamations extensively and sometimes illegally, and that the punishments imposed by the proclamations issued under his protectorship were particularly severe.[51] Autocratic by temperament, Somerset was to run Edward's government as a private fiefdom, using his own men and rewarding them from the king's coffers.

V — GOVERNMENT

Much of what Somerset and his council did in 1547 closely resembled what Henry had been doing in the last years of his reign. There was no sharp break even in religious matters — the Injunctions of 31 July 1547 were very similar to those issued in 1536 and 1538, for example — and the government remained preoccupied by problems of finance and defence.

The foreign situation was, indeed, threatening. In 1545 the English had seized from the French the strategically important port of Boulogne, which, by a treaty of 1546, they were permitted to keep for eight years. However, some aspects of the treaty, and, in particular, the future of another vital port, Calais, remained unresolved at Henry's death. With the death of Francis I on 31 March 1547, the resumption of formal war became almost inevitable, for the new king, Henry II, was determined to avenge the loss of Boulogne. Moreover, with his accession the influence of the Guise family grew, and so, too, did the likelihood of French intervention in the north, the dread of all English monarchs, for the Dowager Queen of Scotland was also a Guise.

51 R. W. Heinze, *The Proclamations of the Tudor Kings* (Cambridge, 1976), 201-23.

The situation in Scotland was complicated by the fact that in 1543 Edward had been betrothed to the infant queen of Scotland, a union that promised to bring to an end centuries of conflict. However, in the event, neither the betrothal nor the treaty of which it was a part had secured stability in Scotland, and armed conflict remained endemic. Desultory negotiations took place throughout the summer of 1547, the English still, publicly at least, putting their faith in the marriage treaty which, they said, would 'knit into one nation' themselves and the Scots. But all parties were meanwhile preparing for hostilities, and in the late summer Somerset led a vast army into Scotland, where, on 10 September, he won a notable victory at Pinkie.[52]

In the months after Pinkie, Somerset was in a position of great strength. Parliament, summoned for November, eased the government's financial difficulties by a statute permitting Edward to dissolve the chantries, whilst the bill repealing Henry VIII's treason legislation on the grounds that 'lighter garments' were more suitable now that 'tempest or winter no longer threatened shows how confident the government felt in its own ability to govern.

Somerset's personal position was strengthened by another bill of repeal, which abolished the curious statute of 1536 whereby future kings could suppress by letters patent any statutes passed before they reached the age of twenty-four, and also by letters patent of 3 November confirming his pre-eminence; this document was signed before the end of the parliamentary session by all the peers who were present for the parliamentary session, by most members of the council, by thirteen bishops and by all the principal legal officers.

Nonetheless, there were clouds on the horizon. Despite the government's caution in religious matters, radicals in London and the home counties took it upon themslves to

52 For a very full account of the battle, see W. Seymour, *Ordeal by Ambition: An English Family in the Shadow of the Tudors* (London, 1972), chapter 10.

abolish all images, and not just those 'abused', as the Injunctions had intended; their actions, and the conservative reaction to them, seriously threatened law and order in some cities. The government attempted to control the situation by a statute 'against such as shall unreverently speak against the sacrament', but in the end it had no option but formally to abolish all images. This horrified traditionalists such as Gardiner.

Law and order were also under threat from other quarters. One threat came from very near at hand: Somerset's brother, Thomas, aggrieved since the time of Henry's death about his elder brother's pre-eminence, began to plot against him.[53] Thomas, who had married with unseemly haste Henry's widow, Catherine Parr, and then, with even more unseemly haste, taken to flirting with the young Princess Elizabeth, who was living with her, was clearly a man of some charm, all of which he employed in his dealings with his young nephew. Through various chamber officials, he constantly sought access to the boy, flattering him and giving him presents and extra pocket money.

From the establishment of the Protectorship Seymour had asserted — with some truth — that in minorities of the past it had been unknown, when the king had two uncles, for one to 'have all rule and the other none, but that if one were protector, the other should be governor'. His bid to secure control of the king's person seems to have been backed, albeit cautiously, by Edward himself, who probably thought that Seymour would make a more enjoyable guardian than did the aloof Somerset; 'my Uncle off Somerset dealeth very hardly with me and keepeth me so straight that I cane not have money at my will', he declared, 'but my Lord Admiral both sends me money and gives me money'.[54]

53 For a full account see G. Bernard, 'The downfall of Sir Thomas Seymour', in *The Tudor Nobility*, ed. G. W. Bernard (Manchester, 1992), 212-40.
54 Bernard, 'The downfall of Sir Thomas Seymour', 220.

But Seymour's machinations did not stop with the young king. He also began to build up support amongst the peerage, to assemble quantities of men and weapons, and to fortify the castle of Holt. On 17 January 1549 he was arrested, interrogated, and then attainted by act of parliament. He was executed on 19 March.

Later, Elizabeth I was to recall that Somerset had told her

> that if his brother had been suffered to speak with him, he had never suffered; but the persuasions were made to him so great, that he was brought in belief that he could not live safely if the Admiral lived; and that made him give his consent to his death.[55]

However, there is no contemporary evidence to suggest that the Protector bemoaned his brother's death, and he certainly signed the death warrant. Yet, whilst it is an exaggeration to claim, as Jordan does, that Thomas Seymour's death 'did grave, perhaps irreparable damage to Somerset's reputation and position', there is ample evidence that both Protector and council felt uneasy in the early spring of 1549. Hugh Latimer preached a number of sermons denigrating Seymour as a man 'the furthest from the fear of God that ever I knew or heard of in England'; he tried hard to justify the government's actions, and, in particular, its decision to proceed by bill of attainder rather than by allowing Seymour a common law trial.

The other major threat to law and order lay in the agrarian situation. Although harvests were good in 1547 and 1548, and grain prices correspondingly low, agrarian discontent was widespread, and manifested itself in frequent violence. The 1540s were a time of great population increase, and increased population led to increased land use. Increased land use often led to tensions, riots and complaints.[56] Preachers and moralists took up these complaints.

55 Jordan, *The Young King*, 381-2.
56 R. B. Manning, *Village Revolts. Social Protest and Popular Disturbances in England 1509-1640* (Oxford, 1988).

They saw the problem as evidence of moral turpitude, arguing, as William Forrest did, that it was the greediness of rack-renting landlords that caused depopulation and unemployment. Such comments obviously influenced the government[57] which, on 1 June 1548, issued a proclamation instituting a 'view or enquiry' into the extent to which existing legislation on tillage was being maintained. The government explained its concern as a response to the desire of the industrious poor for work, to the *pitiful complaints* of the king's poor subjects, and to the comments of *wise and discreet men*, but it may well be that the defence considerations also mentioned in the proclamation — the realm, it was argued, needed *force of men*, not *droves of beasts* — were, in the circumstances of the time, a more telling consideration.

The first commission, covering Oxfordshire, Berkshire, Warwickshire, Leicestershire, Bedfordshire, Buckinghamshire and Northamptonshire, was named on the day of the proclamation. It consisted of local gentlemen, and was chaired by one of the government's financial civil servants, John Hales, a clerk who had risen in the service of Thomas Cromwell and was now an intimate of Somerset. The council clearly intended to appoint a number of other commissions, but it is not known whether it did so. The commissioners were instructed to summon juries of twelve, and enquire of them about the decay of tillage, the keeping of flocks of sheep of 2000 or more, and about emparkment.

The Midland commission speedily set to work; on 23 July Hales told Somerset that he had covered nearly the whole of his circuit, finding the people in general quiet. But Hales was a difficult man, given to provocative statements about the duties and weaknesses of the rich, a habit which did not endear him to the local gentry and nobility. Although he seems to have been careful to tell juries that neither they nor their neighbours should 'go about to ... be executors of the statutes; to cut up men's hedges, and to put

---

57 For a brief account, see W. R. D. Jones, *The Tudor Commonwealth, 1529-1559* (London, 1970) 67.

down their enclosures', he also declared, as moralists such as Forrest and Robert Crowley had done, that 'the people of this realm . . . is greatly decayed through the greediness of a few men', and that God forbids 'the rich to oppress the poor'. By 21 August Somerset was warning Hales that the people,

> whether it be by any words by you to them uttered, wh[ich] they have taken the more encouragement, or else by some other upstirs, are at this present in a marvellous trade of boldness . . . for, whether because of the actions of the commissioners or not, there were indeed a number of stirs in the summer of 1548.

However, in the autumn the country became quieter. Parliament sat from November 1548 to March 1549. In addition to some highly important legislation regulating the church — clergymen were, in future to be allowed to marry, the number of holy-days was reduced, and a new prayer book was authorised — parliament also considered a number of bills dealing with agrarian matters. Hales himself introduced three bills; one, dealing with milk cattle, was rejected, and the other two, controlling tillage and regrating, failed; Hales subsequently compared the fate of his 'programme' bitterly to committing a lamb to a wolf.[58] However, another of Hales's projects was more successful. A new form of taxation was introduced, involving a levy on sheep; this has sometimes been interpreted as a device for limiting the size of flocks, but it seems more probable that it sprang from a concern in government circles about the decline in revenue from wool and woollens.[59] One private bill of the session is also of interest; this was a bill providing that all the Duke of Somerset's tenants should hold 'in the book or roll'.[60] Although the number of tenants affected by

---

[58] See Hales' 'Defence', printed in E. Lamond, ed., *A Discourse of the Common Weal of the Realm of England* (Cambridge, 1929), lxii-iii; Bush, *Government Policy*, 49-51.

[59] Bush, *Government Policy*, 52-3.

[60] See I. S. Leadam, 'The Security of Copyholders in Fifteenth and Sixteenth Century England', *EHR*, 8 (1893); E. Kerridge, *Agrarian Problems in the Sixteenth Century and After* (London, 1969), 86-9; Bush, *Government Policy*, 55-6.

the bill was not great, and the improvement in their legal position only relative, the passing of the act does suggest that Somerset took seriously the advice he gave to others about putting their own houses in order.

With milder weather, unrest surfaced again, encouraged by a widespread misunderstanding of the government's position. In early May 1549, for example, a crowd at Frome in Wiltshire pulled down hedges and fences; those involved told the magistrates who hastily assembled that they had done nothing unlawful, as they knew of a proclamation instructing them 'so do to'. Indeed, the government tacitly admitted its own responsibility in a proclamation of 23 May which ordered an end to rioting, and condemned those who 'under pretence' of the earlier proclamation were destroying 'pales, hedges and ditches at their will and pleasure'. Another proclamation, of 14 June, promised pardon to rioters, recognising that they had been misled by the earlier proclamation.

Despite the unrest, the council on 8 July took the extraordinary step of establishing a fresh commission: moreover, whereas the 1548 commission had been intended, in Hales's words, 'only to inquire, and not to here and determine', the new commissioners were told that if they discovered any commons or highways to have been enclosed or emparked 'contrary to right and without due recompense, that then the same shall be reformed by the said commissiners'. The issuing of the second enclosure commission was the more astonishing because the minor agrarian disturbances of 1548 and early 1549 had by this time turned into something infinitely more substantial: rebellion.

VI — THE REBELLIONS OF 1549

What became the first major rising of 1549 had begun on Whit Monday, 10 June, at the Devon village of Sampford Courtenay. On the previous day, Whit Sunday, the Edwardian Prayer Book, sanctioned by parliament in the preceding winter, had come into use. On the Sunday the villagers at Sampford had allowed their priest, William Harper, to conduct services in accordance with the new order, but when he attempted to use the Prayer Book again on the Monday, his congregation instead forced him to put on his 'old popish attire', and celebrate mass in Latin. The unrest spread to Crediton, and then to Clyst St. Mary. By late June all north Devon was disturbed, and Cornwall had joined in. On 2 July, the rebels laid siege to Exeter.

Somerset was in despair. Not only was the south-west in revolt, risings also occurred in Oxfordshire and Buckinghamshire. Writing to lord Russell, whom the council had dispatched to deal with the siege of Exeter, Somerset declared: 'we had determined to send down to you the Lord Grey, with a band of horsemen' and some soldiers,

> but that upon occasion of a stir here in Buckinghamshire and Oxfordshire by instigation of sundry priests (keep it to yourself), for these matters of religion, we have been forced to keep him a while . . . [61]

For a week or so the situation in Oxfordshire was shaky, until Grey defeated the rebels at the battle of Enslow Hill. On 16 August, lord Russell lifted the siege of Exeter, and, the next day, crushed the remaining insurgents at the battle of Sampford Courtenay.

What had provoked the rising in the south-west? There is little direct evidence about motivation, beyond the lists of rebels' grievances, which have, as always, to be treated with some caution. However, the striking thing about all versions is their concentration on religious issues. As well as complaining about changes in the church's practices over baptism and confirmation, the rebels asked for the sacrament to be administered to the laity in one kind only, and that it should be reserved. They demanded the restoration of holy

---

61 ed. N. Pocock, *Troubles connected with the Prayer Book of 1549*, Camden Society, old series, 34 (1884), 26.

bread and holy water, images and 'all other ancient old cere-monies'. They wanted the doctrine of transubstantiation to be re-asserted, and the act of six articles restored. Throughout, the articles breathed a marked contempt for the new Prayer Book, described as a 'Christmas game' and a 'Christmas play'.

Only a very few articles dealt with grievances other than religious ones. The rebels claimed that the Cornish men could not understand the English of the new Prayer Book, and demanded, rather puzzlingly, that the number of ser-vants kept by gentlemen should be restricted. They also raised the newly-introduced tax on sheep and cloth, and the problem of dearth. None of this adds up to an overall eco-nomic and social explanation of the rising: religion was, clearly, the main driving force of the risings in the south-west and the Thames Valley.

The other major rising of 1549 had no such strong reli-gious component, although it began, in early June, with a riot at Wymondham amongst those assembled for a play to mark the anniversary of the translation of Thomas Becket. By 12 July it had become a full-blown rising, with rebels encamped on Mousehold Heath, just outside Norwich. The rising soon spread to other places in Norfolk, with camps at Castle Rising, King's Lynn and Downham Market, and into Suffolk, where there were camps at Bury St. Edmunds, Melton and Ipswich.[62] There was also trouble in adjoining counties; in Cambridgeshire, Essex, Lincolnshire and Kent. An attempt to crush the rising on 31 July by William Parr, marquis of Northampton, was ignominiously unsuccessful, and it was not until 24 August that the earl of Warwick was able to assemble sufficient men, including a small number of German mercenaries, to put down the Norfolk camp.

Although the rising began with the throwing down of some hedges — Robert Kett's 'close' at Wymondham, and

62 D. MacCulloch, 'Kett's Rebellion in Context', *Past and Present*, 84 (1979).

then that of his arch-enemy, the lawyer turned squire, John Flowerdew, there is little evidence that actual enclosure was a problem in the area. Indeed, the only — and highly ambiguous — mention of enclosure in the rebels' articles may well suggest that enclosure was acceptable when undertaken for the farming of saffron. The main thrust of the rebels' grievances was an anxiety about the over-use of land, and in particular the over-use of common land, and a belief that corruption and the pursuit of self-interest had seriously undermined the ability of the gentry to administer the area. The articles drawn up at the camp on Mousehold Heath also complained about potential or real increases in prices and rents; they asked, for example, that copyhold lands should be charged at the death of a tenant or at the time of sale, with 'an easy fine such as a capon'.

What do the events of 1549 tell us about England in Edward's reign? The happenings of 1549 make it clear that there was considerable resistance to religious change in many parts of the kingdom. They also show that the forces of repression were not, at the county level, very well organised — indeed, Russell suggested that the situation in the south-west had come about partly as a result of the 'lack of good orders amongst such as ought to rule the Commons'. And, above all, the events of 1549 tell us that not all was well with central government.

VII — THE AFTERMATH OF THE RISINGS

The events of 1549 raise a number of important questions about central government. Firstly, was it in any way responsible for the risings? Secondly, did it handle the crisis properly? Thirdly, how united was the government in its approach to the country's problems?

As far as the Western Rising and the other protests against the new Prayer Book are concerned, there can be no doubt that the Protector and council had sanctioned, and, indeed, encouraged, religious change; in the debates which had taken place before the first formal reading of the new Book in parliament at the end of 1548 only three laymen had taken part, but these three — Somerset, Warwick and the secretary to the council, Smith — were all part of the government and all hostile to the conservative position. It may be that events in London and the home counties, where the radicals were in the ascendant, had misled the government into a belief that the country as a whole was more in favour of change than it actually was.

It may also be that the Protector and council believed that the new Prayer Book, with its various theological ambiguities, was unlikely to produce popular resistance; after all, even the conservative Gardiner said that he could use it (although in the event he did not). However, the fact is that whatever the doctrines taught in the Book — and these may have been unclear even to many of the clergy — its message about ceremonies was unambiguous: they were to be drastically reduced. Irrespective of its doctrinal position, the Book involved, visually and orally, a great break with tradition. Not surprisingly, then, it was much disliked in traditionalist areas.

The Prayer Book was, then, a misjudgment; it was a misjudgment for which Cranmer was largely responsible — the principles enshrined in the Book, like the language it uses, are his — but other members of the government, and, indeed, parliament, had concurred in its implementation. The risings of 1549 therefore discredited Cranmer's moderate and piecemeal approach to reform, leaving him vulnerable to more extreme reformers, and left the Protector exposed to attack both by those who felt that no change should take place in the church during a minority and by those who felt that nothing less than whole-hearted protestantism would serve.

In his journal the young king suggested that the agrarian risings of 1549 began 'because certain commissions were went down to pluck down enclosures', and other contemporaries also blamed the commissioners, and their supposed author, Somerset, for the violence. However, as Hales pointed out, there had been risings in Hertfordshire 'before this commission was sent forth', and many risings took place in counties where no commissions had operated. But there did exist in 1549 a widespread belief that the government was sympathetic to the plight of the lower orders, and this belief itself encouraged violence: as we have seen, the Frome rioters declared that they were acting legally, and so did many others. In September 1549 one gentleman declared acidly that a rascal could be found

> in very town and tippling house, my lord's grace [i.e., Somerset's] name in his mouth, saying that his grace had allowed all his doings for good, and in every town and village receiving bills of complaint of divers of this sort.[63]

Was this popular belief that the Protector sympathised with the rebels totally erroneous?

On several occasions Somerset was recorded as having expressed sympathy with the protestors. Hales said that the Protector had declared in August 1548 that despite 'the devil, private profit, self-love, money and suchlike the devil's instruments', the commission should go forward, and the tone of his own letters to Somerset in the summer of 1548 exhibits a confident belief that the Protector shared his aims and beliefs. The usually well-informed imperial ambassadors reported on 13 June 1549 that the Protector had told his colleagues on the council that

> the peasants' demands were fair and just; for the poor people who had no land to graze their cattle ought to retain the commons and the lands that had always been public property, and the noble and the rich ought not to seize and add them to their parks and possessions,

63 B. L. Beer and R. J. Nash, 'Hugh Latimer and Lusty Knave of Kent; the Commonwealth Movement of 1549', *Bulletin of the Institute of Historical Research*, 52 (1979), 175-8.

and only a month later Paget wrote complaining about the Protector's liking for the prayers of the poor.[64] Thus, his colleagues' subsequent complaint that Somerset had often declared that 'the people had good cause to reform . . . things themselves' is substantiated by earlier evidence.

Somerset has, in fact, been credited by some historians with the encouragement of a group of 'common-wealth' preachers and moralists who were anxious both to promote social reform and to advance the cause of protestantism; W. R. D. Jones, for instance, in his *The Tudor Commonwealth, 1529-1559*, writes of a 'Commonwealth Party which looked to Somerset for patronage and included in it John Hales and a number of divines such as Latimer and Lever'.[66] However, the evidence for the existence of such a group and for Somerset's active encouragement of it are alike tenuous. Although we can perhaps describe as 'commonwealth' the assumptions and rhetorical expressions frequently used in the middle of the sixteenth century by preachers and pamphleteers of a more radical persuasion, no commonwealth 'movement' or 'party' eisted in this period in any organised or coherent form,[67] and Somerset's personal links with the men who most frequently expressed such ideas were limited. Of those he has known to have personally patronised, only Hales and Becon, who wrote in *The jewel of joy* that 'the cause of all this wretchedness and beggary in the commonwealth are the greedy gentlemen, which are sheep-mongers and graziers', can be described as having commonwealth tendencies. Yet Hales himself explicitly stated that he knew nothing of the setting up of the enclosure commission before he was named as a commissioner, and there is no evidence to link Becon with the formulation of government policy. The majority of those usually described as belonging to the commonwealth movement were either court preachers, like

64 Strype, *Ecclesiastical Memorials*, VI, 420.

66 Jones, *Tudor Commonwealth*, 32.

67 G. R. Elton, 'Reform and the "Commonwealthmen" of Edward VI's Reign', in P. Clark, A. G. R. Smith, and N. Tyache, eds. *The English Commonwealth, 1547-1640* (London, 1979).

Latimer, whose links were chiefly with Cranmer, or were without any government affiliations at all; thus, Robert Crowley, perhaps the most prolific of the Edwardian pamphleteers, was a stationer and book-seller before being ordained in 1551.

It is true that commonwealth expressions did find their way into some government documents of this period; a proclamation of April 1549, for example, condemned the greediness of men who were 'blind and ignorant in brotherly love and charity, that ought to be between Christian man and Christian man, and the natural love and amity of one Englishman to another'. But such phrases were no more than the rhetorical small-change of the period; they had been used by Wolsey in 1527, and continued to be employed until the Civil War.[68]

However, although Somerset was never the leader of a party committed to social and religious reform, he was more sympathetic to the plight of the lower orders than some of his colleagues thought wise. Although there is no reason to assume that the initial establishment of the enclosure commission was the work of Somerset alone — only one councillor, the earl of Warwick, is known to have expressed reservations in the summer of 1548, and even he subsequently agreed to it — the risings of early 1549 alarmed a number of Somerset's colleagues, and made them doubt the wisdom of his policy. On 7 July 1549 Paget wrote from Brussels advising the Protector that if the whole council urged something, he should give way: 'I know in this matter of the Commons', he said,

> every man of the council have misliked your proceedings . . . would to God, that, at the first stir you had followed the matter hotly, and caused justice to be ministered in solemn fashion to the terror of others . . .[69]

But Somerset ignored Paget's advice.

68 P. A. Slack, 'Dearth and Social Policy in Early Modern England', *Social History of Medicine*, 5 (1992), 5-9.
69 Strype, *Ecclesiastical Memorials*, VI, 421-3.

What of the government's handling of the crisis of 1549? It had been neither fast nor effective, in part at least because of the co-incidence of popular rising and foreign threats. But most of the difficulty lay in the Protector's personality. Somerset's reaction to the crisis had not been well-judged. His temper had soured; he shouted at his colleagues and contemptuously ignored their advice. He blamed his commanders in the field for their shortages of men and armaments. He also issued a series of occasionally contradictory proclamations that seemed to justify the rebels' actions. His fellow councillors began to plot against him, and, finally, in early October, they overthrew him.[70]

VIII — THE FALL OF THE PROTECTOR

On 5 October the young king publicly summoned 'all his loving subjects' to repair to Hampton Court 'with harness and weapon', to defend him and the Protector. On the same day a letter was sent in the king's name to Henry Seymour, the Protector's younger brother, informing him about 'a carton conspiracy' and ordering him to levy men and bring them to court. Somerset himself wrote to one of his servants urging the earl of Oxford to be ready to assist the king, and he sent his son to Lord Russell and Sir William Herbert, who were still on their way back from the south-west, with a letter begging them to come to his aid.

What had alarmed the Protector was an assembly of his council colleagues in the capital — as they later said, disingenuously, 'as soon as he heard that certain of the Lords of the Council had met and consulted together', he had begun to levy troops. The Protector had correctly diagnosed what was going on. The councillors in the capital, later known as

70 For an argument that the plot to overthrow the Protector began early in the summer of 1549, see J. Berkman, 'Van der Delft's Letter. A Reappraisal of the Attack on Protector Somerset', *Bulletin of the Institute of Historical Research*, 1980.

'the London lords', startled the citizens by going around armed, and 'their servants likewise weaponed, attending upon them in new liveries'. Somerset, who hastily moved with the king to the fortified castle of Windsor, was informed that there were at least two thousand horsemen on the streets of the capital.

For some days claim and counter-claim were exchanged. The councillors in London drafted aggrieved statements, rejecting the Protector's 'falsehoods', and expounding their own position. Hand-bills urging the people to rise and save the Duke were also circulated; if these were produced by Somerset or his supporters, which is not certain, they were counter-productive, alienating and offending the propertied and socially-conservative. The Protector became increasingly isolated; on 9 October the city authorities threw in their lot with the London lords, and Somerset's last hope, Russell and Herbert, soon did the same. On 12 October the London lords, confident of success, set off for Windsor. Somerset surrendered without bloodshed, and he and the king came back to London on 14 October — Somerset to the Tower. Interrogated by his former colleagues, Somerset soon 'confessed' to a list of twenty-nine articles laid against him; these formed the basis of a statute 'for the fine an ransom' of the duke, passed by parliament the following January.

Was this the tragic overthrow of a liberal and compassionate statesman as Jordan, for instance, would have us believe? Should we set the October coup firmly against the murky background of sixteenth-century power politics, and look in particular to the ambition of the earl of Warwick? Or can the change of government be justified by the charges laid against the Protector?

Most of the information we have about the coup's objectives was produced during and after the event, to justify what had been done, and it must therefore be treated with some caution. In particular, the lords' assertion that they had made some kind of contract with Somerset at the beginning of his Protectorship, when, they said, he had promised 'that he should do nothing touching the state of the affairs of his highness without the advice and consent of the rest of the council', and the suggestion that they had throughout the period of the Protectorship been unhappy about some aspects of Somerset's behaviour, need to be regarded with scepticism. Paget's letters of advice show no evidence of serious splits between the Protector and the other councillors before the spring of 1549 — and this despite the fact that Paget was temperamentally inclined to pessimism. But in a letter of May 1549 Paget complained that whereas in the past the Protector had listened to him 'very gently and graciously' at the council table, now he was prone to 'nip' sharply, and he also related how Sir Richard Lee, a prominent military engineer, had been reduced to tears when Somerset had 'very sore, and too much more than needed, rebuked him'.[71] By early June, Paget's letters reflect a disastrously divided council.[72]

But even if the justifications of the London lords do not tell the whole truth, they are, nonetheless, revealing. They suggest, for example, that foreign affairs were very much more in the councillors' minds than historians have traditionally implied — indeed, the first charge laid against Somerset by the London lords in their proclamation of 8 October is that he had risked the overseas possessions so hard won by Henry VIII. The London lords' accounts also show us a Somerset very different from Pollard and Jordan's commonwealth-inspired dreamer: they speak of a man openly contemptuous of his colleagues, a man who was systematically packing the offices of state with his own followers, a man given to 'alchemy and multiplication' — that is, embezellment — and to 'fantastical and unnecessary buildings'.

71 Strype, *Ecclesiastical Memorials*, VI, 418.
72 Strype, *Ecclesiastical Memorials*, VI, 423.

How legitimate do these four main charges — misconduct of foreign affairs, bad handling of the council, factionalism, and extravagance — look in the light of subsequent researches?

The vast majority of English — and, indeed, American — historians working on this period have been much more interested in domestic affairs than they have been in foreign, but in fact Edward's government was, for most of this period, preoccupied by events abroad, and, in particular, with Scotland and France.

It is initially surprising to find Somerset, the victor of Pinkie, charged with the unsatisfactory conduct of foreign affairs. After all, so concerned with Scotland had Somerset been that it is possible for one historian, M. L. Bush, to argue that his attack on greedy landlords was a mere ploy, intended to distract attention from the pernicious effects of currency debasement — debasement being the only means by which the duke's expensive garrisoning policy could be financed. But the truth is that despite Pinkie and the failure of the Scots to capture even such exposed positions as Broughty Castle, the English cause had not prospered in Scotland. In January 1548 the Scots had begun to discuss a marriage between their young queen and the Dauphin; six months later, a substantial French expeditionary force landed at Leith, and removed Mary to France. Somerset had planned an offensive campaign for the summer of 1549, but the major rebellions of that year necessitated the withdrawal of troops to the south-west and Norfolk. The French seized their opportunity, and on 8 August 1549, Henry II declared war on England, and took personal command of the troops outside Boulogne.

Against this background of stale-mate in Scotland, and war with France, the charges levelled at Somerset become more comprehensible. He was criticised for the loss of Haddington and Newhaven, and for the fact that Boulogne and the territories roundabout were in danger. It was also claimed that Somerset 'would not suffer the king's pieces beyond the seas, called Newhaven and Blacknes, to be furnished with men and victuals, although [he] was advertised of the faults therein by the captains of the said pieces and others'.

Two things give some substance to these complaints. First is the fact that very large sums had been spent during the Protectorate — perhaps £200,000 p.a. on Scotland alone[73] — without any obvious improvement in England's long-term prospects in either France or Scotland. Secondly, a high proportion of the actions taken by the London lords immediately after Somerset's surrender concerned defence — the army's arrears were paid, for example, and Sir Richard Cotton, once treasurer at Boulogne, was sent off to the Scottish border. Warwick was created Lord Admiral, and the ambassadors to the emperor, Sir Thomas Cheye and Sir Philip Hoby, were instructed to seek aid from him for the defence of Boulogne. Foreign affairs were clearly, for the council, very important.

What of the claim that Somerset had mis-handled the council? Although the charge that he

> sometime rebuked, checked and taunted, as well privately as openly, divers of the . . . councillors, for showing and declaring their advice and opinion against his purposes [74]

must, since it was not made until after his fall, be treated with some scepticism, Somerset was certainly not a good committee man. Although he was unwilling to apply his mind to matters in which he had little interest, such as finance, he was also reluctant to delegate, as Paget frequently pointed out.[75] In consequence, vital matters were neglected; at Christmas 1548, for example, Paget told the

---

73 Bush, *Government Policy*, chapter 9.

74 Foxe, *Acts and Monuments*, VI, 290.

75 See, for example, his letter of 12 March 1549, in *The Letters of William, Lord Paget of Beaudesert, 1547-63* ed. B. L. Beer and S. M. Jack, *Camden Miscellany*, XXV (1974), 267.

Protector that those in parliament were puzzled by his slowness in introducing a subsidy bill.[76]

Indeed, recent research has tended to substantiate the councillors' complaints. Somerset often ignored the privy council; as Dale Hoak has shown, the written record of meetings during his period of power is largely fictitious, and most administration was done without consultation in the Protector's own household.[77] The reports of the Imperial ambassador, van der Delft, also show that even on occasions when he had been invited formally to address the whole council, the really significant discussions were conducted in subsequent tête-à-têtes with the Protector alone. Indeed, as early as May 1547, van der Delft had reported that 'all solicitation and resort are at the Protector's palace [maison] where the Council meet and all business is despatched'.

As well as criticising Somerset's conduct of business, the London lords claimed that he had advanced his own clients to an improper extent; in particular, he was charged with having dismissed existing justices in order to put in his own men.[78] The charge is difficult to substantiate, but it is of interest that a number of Somerset's close associates became justices of the peace for the first time in 1547. Those promoted to the bench in 1547 included Somerset's receiver-general, John Berwick, his auditor, Matthew Colhurst, his servant, William Gray, and Sir Ralph Vane, who was to be executed with the duke in 1552. Somerset also pushed his protégés more generally in the counties. Thus, in Wiltshire he advanced John Bonham, 'his one hand', and in Gloucestershire 'his other hand', Sir Miles Partridge; Partridge was to be indicted in January 1552, with Somerset's brother-in-law, Sir Michael Stanhope, for 'holding rebellious assemblies', and he was subsequently exe-

76 Printed by B. L. Beer in 'A Critique of the Protectorate: An Unpublished Letter of Sir William Paget to the Duke of Somerset', *Huntington Library Quarterly*, 34 (1970-1), 277-83.
77 Hoak, *King's Council*, 15-23, 112-6.
78 Pocock, *Troubles*, LIII, LX.

cuted. In Devon, Piers Courtenay, who was sheriff in 1549, was described as Somerset's 'minister'.

Somerset also placed his own clients in some key positions at court. In August 1547, for example, he made Sir Michael Stanhope groom of the stole; by the next year Stanhope was recognised as one of the chief gentlemen of the privy chamber. By virtue of this role Stanhope could control the young king for Somerset; he, after all, held 'the privy key', kept the dry stamp and administered the king's personal revenues.[79] In so doing Stanhope advanced his own position as well as that of his brother-in-law; he piled up fees, salaries and offices, and he was able to snap up quantities of chantry land.

What of the charges about Somerset's extravagance — what, for instance, about the 'pompous building' and the accusation levelled by the London lords in their proclamation of 8 October that Somerset, 'in all this time of the wars built most sumptuously in a number of places, the King's Majesty's poor Soldiers . . . unpaid'?[80] At Somerset House, in the Strand, the Protector built what has been described as 'unquestionably one of the most influential buildings of the English Renaissance';[81] its relatively low height, its use of stone, the superimposed orders, and the relationship of the parts all 'represent the new direction in architecture'.[82] He also constructed, in the same area, Somerset Yard, Somerset Stairs, and Somerset Wharf. To clear the ground for these, he levelled the church of St. Mary le Strand, and 'Strand Inne, Strand Bridge with the lane vnder it, the Bishop of Chesters Inne [an Inn of Chancery[83]], the Bishoppe of Worcesters Inne, with all the tenamentes adioyning'.[84] He

79 D. E. Hoak, 'The King's Privy Chamber, 1547-1553', in *Tudor Rule and Revolution*, ed. DeLloyd Guth and J. McKenna (London, 1982) 105-6.

80 Pocock, *Troubles*, LIII. See also S. Brigden, *London and the Reformation* (Oxford, 1989), 496.

81 Summerson, 45.

82 M. Howard, *The Early Tudor Country House. Architecture and Politics, 1490-1550* (London, 1987), 194.

83 Stow, I, 77.

84 J. Stow, *A Survey of London*, ed. C. L. Kingsford (Oxford, 1908), II, 93.

pulled down most of the church of St. John of Jerusalem, including the great Bell Tower, for its stone,[85] and on 10 April 1549 destroyed a chapel at St. Paul's, with 'the whole Cloister, the dance of Death, the Tombs and Monuments; so that nothing was left but the bare plot of ground'.[86] In the process, Somerset also destroyed the charnel house, which resulted in a thousand cart loads of bones being dumped on Finsbury Fields. He had his eye on the stone of St. Margaret's, Westminster — now the church of the House of Commons — but his fall came before he could demolish that.

Somerset began the conversion of the Bridgettine nunnery he had acquired at Isleworth, Syon, into a great brick courtyard house.[87] He planned to replace his family home, Wulf Hall, with something much grander; during 1548 and the early part of 1549 considerable preparatory works were completed, involving nearly three hundred men and two million bricks.[88] Work was also carried out at Berry Pomeroy Castle, in Devon,[89] and at Banbury, Odiham and Reading. Indeed, so extensive were the Protector's building activities that he set up a works organisation 'similar in its hierarchial complexity to that of the Royal Works'.[90]

On his building projects, Somerset spent enormous sums. He used Henry VIII's master carver, William Cave, for his building, as well as the royal painter, Nicholas de Modena, and both the materials and the furnishings were of the best; in September 1548, for example, four ships were laden in France with Caen stone for the Protector's buildings, and 'marble pillars' were sent from Flanders for Somerset House. In three years the Protector expended

85 Stow, II, 84-5. Cardinal Pole repaired the church in the next reign.

86 Stow, I, 328.

87 Howard, *The early Tudor Country House*, 188, 211.

88 Jackson, 'Wulf Hall and the Seymours', 181.

89 Howard, *The Early Tudor Country House*, 203.

90 M. Airs, *The Making of the English Country House 1500-1640* (London, 1975), 47. See also p52.

£10,000 on Somerset House alone, another £5,000 on Syon and £2,000 on his other projects. This contrasts interestingly with the three or four hundred pounds he spent in the same period on gifts and charity. Such expenditure could be justified by Somerset's position — he was, after all, entertaining ambassadors and the like. But the question of how he amassed these sums is, obviously, of interest.

In the first year of Edward's reign crown lands with a capital value of £107,712 were given away, mostly to those in power. In this hand-out, Somerset was a substantial beneficiary. As we have seen, great sums were first given out from the royal coffers under Henry VIII's 'unwritten will', and Somerset thus acquired land allegedly worth £800 p.a.[91] He also received other substantial grants. In 1547, for example, he was given land worth nearly £400 p.a. from the temporalities of the see of Lincoln. Later that year he got another grant of lands worth £500 p.a. in gratitude for his victory at Pinkie — this time from the bishopric of Bath and Wells. It is probable that, overall, Somerset in Edward's reign was able to add another £5,000 p.a. to his already substantial income.[92]

It would be difficult to prove that Somerset was any more greedy or corrupt than his fellow-councillors; rather, his opportunities were the greatest. Certainly, however — and this is important for his reputation as 'the good duke' — he seized his opportunities. The charge of 'alchemy and multiplication' cannot be proved, but the judicious historian of Tudor coinage, C. E. Challis, has noted that the establishment of the Durham House mint in 1548 'was from the start a superfluous creation'; Challis therefore supports Thomas Seymour's contention that the Protector had set up the mint for his own purposes.[93] Somerset was said to have kept plate confiscated from the college of St. Stephen's,

91 Miller, 'Henry VIII's unwritten will', 103.
92 Jackson, 'Wulf Hall and the Seymours', 189.
93 Challis, *Tudor Coinage*, 7-8.

Westminster, sharing the vestments of the college with his clients, Sir Ralph Fane and John Thynne. He was also accused of having retained jewels belonging to the duke of Norfolk and to William Sharington, and some of his brother's possessions. The same account suggests that he concealed church lead and stone at Syon, Reading and Glastonbury, and that he, with his clients, Smith and Thynne, had held on to payments made to the king for alum. He was accused of having seized the gift of one thousand marks given by the city of London at the time of Edward's coronation, and, by means of Thynne, of taking money from the customs'. A number of inventories of royal plate show that not only Somerset, but also his duchess and his brother-in-law, made free with royal possession; certainly the duke kept 'a Circlet of gold' made for Anne Boleyn's coronation, and a gold sceptre. According to the chronicler, Stow, Somerset also took books from the Guildhall Library, in 'three Cartes'.[94] So numerous, in fact, were the Protector's goods that it took six men thirteen days to list all his belongings at Syan and Shene at the time of his fall.

Thus, it would appear that the London lords' charges against the Protector had considerable justice: he had, indeed, failed in Scotland and France, he had mishandled his colleagues and the crisis of 1549, and he was both corrupt and greedy. There is no need, then, to see his overthrow as 'the triumph of reaction'. Indeed, few of the articles laid against Somerset related to social matters; other than the clauses relating to the enclosure commission, the only charge made against Somerset which might be held up as evidence of the London lords' harshness towards the lower orders relates to the court of requests which the duke held in his own house.[95] Pollard thought that Somerset had set up

94 J. Stow, *A Survey of London*, ed. C. L. Kingsford (2 vols., Oxford, 1908), I, 275.
95 Foxe, *Acts and Monuments*, VI, 290.

the court 'to afford the poor some chance of justice',[96] and Jordan agreed that Somerset used it to provide 'justice for the poor against the mighty'.[97] However, M. L. Bush has shown that Somerset merely employed a master of requests in his household to funnel to the proper court the petitions that were addressed to the Protectorate rather than to the king.[98] Moreover, only two of the ninety surviving bills addressed to Somerset during the Protectorate dealt with the type of agrarian problems that Pollard and Jordan had in mind. Dr. Bush discovered 'no discernible correlation between [Somerset's] degree of participation and the plaintiff's poverty', and it seems best to place the whole matter firmly in the context of a ruler's traditional duty to see that justice was properly administered; Somerset's colleagues objected to his intervention in legal matters not because he was pushing the rights of the humble against those of the rich, but because it was one of a variety of ways in which he appeared to be claiming a quasi-regal power.

On social matters it would seem, moreover, that Somerset differed from his colleagues in degree rather than kind. There is no evidence that the other councillors were anxious to grind the faces of the poor, merely that they felt that it was necessary to re-establish order before further attention was paid to social ills. The social policy implemented during the Protectorship had been entirely traditional — it involved the enforcement of existing statutes against the decay of tillage and engrossment, and the use of proclamations for pricing and quality control. Even the setting-up of a commission was based on an earlier precedent: Wolsey's investigations of 1517-18, after which action had been taken against 264 persons.[99] Nothing changed with

96 Pollard, *England under Protector Somerset*, 233.

97 Jordan, *The Young King*, 361.

98 M. L. Bush, 'Protector Somerset and requests', *Historical Journal*, 17 (1974), 451-64; Dewar, *Sir Thomas Smith*, 27.

99 J. J. Scarisbrick, 'Cardinal Wolsey and the Common Weal', in *Wealth and Power in Tudor England. Essays presented to S. T. Bindoff* ed. E. W. Ives, R. J. Knecht, J. J. Scarisbrick (London, 1978), 52.

43

Somerset's fall — Warwick, and, indeed, Mary, pursued the same ends in the same way.

Nonetheless, many commentators, including some near-contemporaries, described the coup as the work of one man only — Warwick. Observing the subsequent rise of Somerset's old rival, they interpreted all the events of the Protectorate in the light of Warwick's later power. It is impossible totally to discount such theories. Nonetheless, there are two facts which the careful historian should also remember: firstly, Warwick did not become pre-eminent until some months after Somerset's fall, and secondly, for a time it seemed as if his fortune was very closely linked with that of the discredited Protector.

The most likely outcome of Somerset's fall appeared to be the predominance of a 'catholic' party led by the earls of Arundel and Southampton, perhaps with the Princess Mary as Regent.[100] Many contemporaries interpreted the events of October 1549 as a catholic backlash — in Oxford, for example, the conservatives were so cock-a-hoop that Peter Martyr found it prudent to withdraw from the city, whilst Gardiner, still in prison, confidently believed that his release was imminent. As early in the coup as 8 October the London lords had found it necessary to reassure the mayor and aldermen of London assembled in the Guildhall that the seditious rumours circulating to the effect that they would 'reduce matters of religion to the state they were in before' were untrue. A proclamation of 30 October sought to quash rumours that 'the good laws made for religion should be now altered and abolished, and the old Romish service, mass and ceremonies eftsoons renewed and reviewed', but unsuccessfully, since another proclamation, on Christmas Day, noted that

100 Hoak, *King's Council*, 241.

divers unquiet and evil disposed persons, since the apprehension of the Duke of Somerset, have noised and bruited abroad that they should like to have again their old Latin service, their conjured bread and water, with such like vain and superstitious ceremonies . . .

In his New Year's gift to the disgraced duke, Somerset's servant, William Grey, declared that 'the papists' were 'never more lusty then they are now'.[101]

Perhaps all this was a simple misunderstanding, perhaps, as a later account suggests, Warwick deliberately fostered the impression of a catholic coup by plotting with all Somerset's enemies, 'as well those that was for religion as other ways'.[102] But if Warwick was at first willing to make common cause with the conservatives, he was then forced by events to throw in his lot with the radicals. This same account suggests that Southampton, anxious to be revenged for his earlier dismissal,[103] decided that he could eliminate the duke and Warwick at the same time: they were 'traitors both; and both is worthy to die', he declared after his examination of Somerset. His colleague, Arundel, concurred, but the ever-cautious Paulet, now the earl of Wiltshire, hastened away and informed Warwick of what was going on; knowing that his fate was bound up with Somerset's, Warwick softened his attitude towards the duke, and, with Cranmer's assistance, petitioned the king on his behalf. In mid-January there was a confrontation between Warwick and his enemies in the council, after which Arundel and Southampton were banished from court. On 2 February 1550 they were turned off the council. (Southampton subsequently died of grief.) Four days later Somerset was released from the Tower, under house arrest and with a recognisance of

101 I owe this reference to Dr. Phillipa Tudor.
102 British Library Additional MS 48126, f8v. Part of this document was published by A. J. A. Malkiewicz, as 'An Eye-Witness's Account of the Coup d'Etat of October 1549', *EHR*, 70 (1955), 600-9.
103 See page 7.

£10,000. On 18 February he received a free pardon from the king, and on 10 April he was restored to the council. These events surely suggest that, as in the last months of Henry VIII's life, Somerset and Warwick had made common cause.

IX — THE DUDLEY ASCENDANCY

On 20 February 1550 Warwick became Lord President of the council. He also persuaded Edward to put his friends into the privy chamber to replace Somerset's discredited followers and to appoint Sir John Gates, another of his clients, as vice-chamberlain of the household and keeper of the dry stamp. But even with this control over the person of the king, Warwick was never secure. One reason for this was economic: whereas Somerset had ruled in a period of comparative prosperity and good harvests, the latter part of the reign was marked by bad harvests, dearth and disease. Moreover, whilst Somerset had, of course, a traditional and widely-recognised claim to authority over his young nephew, Warwick did not. The privy council covered itself by associating the king's uncle closely with all that it did; Somerset was a fairly regular attender at meetings during 1550 and 1551, and he was, therefore, present when a bullying letter was sent to Mary about the attendance of her household at mass, and when Gardiner and George Day, bishop of Chichester, were censured for their conservative views. He played his part in the repression of the popular discontent that was so marked a feature of this period; in July 1550 he went 'to set order' in Oxfordshire, Sussex, Wiltshire and Hampshire, for example, in December 1550 he was given a licence to retain, and in April 1551 he became Lord Lieutenant of Berkshire and Hampshire.

Overall, the council tried hard to reconcile the duke; on 27 April 1550 it agreed to petition the king for the restoration to Somerset of 'all his goods, his debts, and his leases yet ungiven', and on 15 May it decided to ask him to restore the duke to the privy chamber; both requests were granted.

In June 1550 Somerset received a further £500 'of the King's bequests deceased', as did Paulet and Warwick. To tie the members of the council even more firmly together, various alliances were formed; in June 1550, for example, Somerset's daughter, Anne, was married to Warwick's son. However, this attempt to bind together the council's various factions, and thus provide the young king with a wide-based body of advisers, was doomed, for Somerset was constantly plotting to regain power.

In June 1550 one of Somerset's followers, Richard Whalley, receiver of the Court of Augmentations in Yorkshire, recorded a long conversation that he had had with Warwick, who explicitly warned the duke against trying 'to rule and direct the council at will', since his behaviour had led some of his fellow-councillors to believe that Somerset 'taketh and aspireth to have' his former authority again. Rumours began to circulate about Somerset's intentions. In August 1550, for example, a Londoner, Roger Preston, was ordered to lose his ears for speaking 'lewd words' about the former Protector; the words turned out to be a story that Somerset had proclaimed himself king. In February 1551 the council questioned the earl of Rutland about a conversation he had had with Whalley, who was said to have raised with the earl the possibility of restoring Somerset to his former position. At this point the council proceeded no further, but in the autumn more details emerged of this affair. One of Warwick's men, Sir Thomas Palmer, then revealed that Somerset had planned to invite Warwick, Northampton and others to a banquet, to assassinate them and to seize power. The duke was accordingly arrested.

Somerset was indicted under the 1547 treason act on the grounds that by assembling men with the intention of imprisoning Warwick and other councillors he was compassing to deprive the king of his dignity, and was further charged under the 1550 act which had made it a treasonable offence to assemble forces with the intention of murdering or imprisoning a privy councillor. He was tried by his peers in Westminster Hall on 1 December 1551. The Lord Stewart, Winchester, presided over a gathering of twenty-two peers. Evidence against the duke was given by Palmer, by one of his own servants, William Crane, described as a 'man who having consumed his own estate had armed himself to any mischief', and by Whalley. After considerable debate, the court acquitted Somerset of treason, but found him guilty of felony under the third clause of the 1550 act which referred to the bringing together of men for the purpose of a riot.[104] He was condemned to death.

The use of the treason law in this way was dubious, as the court seems to have understood. Moreover, it seems probable that part, at least, of the evidence against Somerset was fabricated: Palmer, a close confidant of Warwick and a known critic of Somerset, was a strange associate for those involved in a plot to restore the former Protector;[105] indeed, one narrative of these years claims that Palmer confessed before his death in 1553 that he had given false evidence. The role and loyalties of Whalley and Rutland are alike unclear.[106]

However, even if he had not committed the precise offences with which he was charged, Somerset may not have been totally innocent of an intention to do Warwick harm, and to regain his own position. A not unsympathetic French account claims that Somerset, from the time of his release from the Tower, made common cause with all malcontents, high and low. This account suggests that the duke let it be known amongst the people that the debasement of the coinage — which caused considerable distress in 1550

104 J. Bellamy, *The Tudor Law of Treason* (London and Toronto, 1979), 244-5.

105 Somerset criticised openly and harshly Palmer's conduct at the siege of Haddington. Palmer supported Warwick in the coup of 1553, and died with him at Tower Hill.

106 Whalley was imprisoned at Somerset's fall, and again, briefly, at the time of Rutland's examination. Arrested in October 1551, he remained in confinement for several months after Somerset's death, and was also fined £1000 for peculation. Released in June 1552, he was put in prison again two months later, where he remained until Mary's accession.

and 1551 — was none of his making, a story corroborated by a report of the Imperial ambassador, Scheyfve, about 'the murmurings of the people against the depreciation of the currency', for which 'some people wished to blame the Earl of Warwick'. Moreover, one of the questions put to the duke in the Tower concerned an attempt to persuade the people to dislike the existing government. The anonymous French account also claims that Arundel and Somerset planned at the next meeting of parliament to assert that

> the realm is very badly governed, the people bur-
> dened with new subsidies, the king poorer than
> ever, officials unpaid. And that the government did
> everything arbitrarily, without any account of the
> constitution and the country's laws.

Interestingly, one of the questions put to Somerset by his interrogators was whether it was he or Arundel (who was arrested in November 1551) who had sought 'to have a parliament'.

Amongst the 'malcontents' with whom Somerset appears to have made common cause were a number of northern magnates. By the autumn of 1550 the earls of Derby and Shrewsbury were out of sympathy with the gov-
ernment in London, and in the spring of 1551 they seem to have come to some agreement with Somerset.[107] Repeatedly summoned to court in the early months of the year, the earls did not arrive until late May and June, and then they were acompanied by an intimidating array of horsemen and other retainers. When Somerset was finally arrested Shrewsbury was questioned about conversations that he had had with Whalley, whilst Derby's son, Lord Strange, was for a time rumoured to be under arrest.

Another northern magnate involved in these machina-
tions was Cuthbert Tunstal, bishop of Durham. Already out of favour because of his opposition to religious change,

107 G. W. Bernard, *The Power of the Early Tudor Nobility. A Study of the Fourth and Fifth Earls of Shrewsbury* (Sussex, 1985), 64-8.

Tunstal was under house-arrest from the autumn of 1550.[108] But in December 1551 a letter about a rising in the north in Tunstal's hand was found amongst Somerset's effects, and the bishop was called to account before the council. His explanation was found unsatisfactory, and a bill to deprive him of his bishopric on grounds of misprision of the treason was subsequently brought into parliament, although it was lost when members of the Commons asked that the bishop should appear in person before them. The whole affair is mysterious, and it may well be that Tunstal's offence was merely technical; nonetheless, the fact remains that a group of discontented elements was beginning, in late 1550 and early 1551, to coalesce around the figure of Somerset.

The role of religious conservatives in these machinations is of interest, for during 1550 and 1551 the imperial ambassadors had frequently suggested that Somerset's zeal for religious change was waning. Such reports may be dismissed as wishful thinking, but there are certain other indications that support them. An exiled French divine, Francis Bourgoyne, told Calvin at the time of Somerset's death that the duke 'had become so lukewarm in the service of Christ as scarcely to have anything less at heart than the state of religion'.[109] Such views were echoed by one of the king's chaplains, John Bradford, who urged those in authority in the latter part of Edward's reign to take note of Somerset's fate,

> who became so cold in hearing God's word, that, the year before his last apprehension, he would go to visit his masons, and would not dingy [i.e., trouble] himself from his gallery to go to his hall for hearing of a sermon'.

108 C. Sturge, *Cuthbert Tunstall: Churchman, Scholar, Statesman, Administrator* (London, 1938), 284-92.

109 *Original Letters*, II, 734.

110 *The Writings of John Bradford*, ed. A. Townsend, I (Parker Society, 1853), 111. It has sometimes been claimed that John Mardeley's words in *Here beginneth a necessarie instruction for all couetouse ryche men* — I builded my houses, orchards & gardens of pleasure' — apply to Somerset, but that work was published in 1548, before the duke's passion for building was manifest, and although Mardeley dedicated another of his books to Edward Seymour, he nowhere in his writings demonstrates any acquaintanceship with the Protector himself.

Perhaps Somerset had become disillusioned, perhaps, as Bourgoyne suggested, his religious views had always been shaped by prudential considerations; 'if it had been more for his interest to have followed a different course, he would at some time or other have made his recantation'.

X — SOMERSET'S DEATH

Nonetheless, Somerset's faith was to sustain him at the time of his death in a way in which Warwick's would not. The night before his execution Somerset wrote various solemn thoughts based on Biblical texts on the fly-leaf of his pocket calendar — the fear of the Lord is the beginning of wisdom, put thy trust in the Lord, fly from evil and so on.[111] He behaved with great courage at his execution on 22 January, speaking at length to a large crowd, some of whom subsequently 'washed their hands in his blood . . . and dipped their handkerchiefs in it'.

John King has described Somerset's conduct and his words as those of a man imitating 'the manner of a Protestant martyr';[112] the duke rejoiced that the state of religion in England now drew near 'unto the form and order of the primitive church', and declared, 'I die here in the faith of Jesus Christ'. However, this protestant emphasis may in fact come from Foxe, whose account of Somerset's speech this is.[113] A different source presents Somerset more as a Christian stoic, claiming: 'I have often looked death in the face in great adventures in the field, he is now no stranger unto me'. He declared: ' I neither fear to die nor desire to live', and asked that no one should 'sorrow' for him. Yet a third account, coming from one of the foreign protestant community, Francis Bourgoyne, has Somerset showing both 'the firmness of a hero, and the modesty of a Christian'.[114]

111 King, *Print, Patronage and Propaganda*, 117-9.
112 Ibid, 119.
113 Foxe, *Acts and Monuments*, VI, 293-5.
114 *Original letters*, 731-3.

Bourgoyne noted that the duke was 'as splendidly attired as he used to be when about to attend upon the king', and that he gave the executioner 'some gold rings which he drew from his fingers'. All accounts agree that Somerset urged obedience to the king and council upon his on-lookers.

Perhaps all the various impressions that Somerset gave at his death were correct, and reflected some part of his personality. The precise form taken by his religious convictions may indeed, as Bourgoyne suggested, have been shaped by prudential considerations, but he nonetheless had a sincere religious conviction which sustained him at the end. Although Somerset was not a bookish man, nor even a well-educated one, he knew enough of the Bible and of the classics to conduct himself properly in the face of death, and he was enough of a soldier to confront his fate unflinchingly. But, above all, he was a Tudor magnate; his last auction was to give his sword to the lieutenant of the Tower.

CONCLUSION

Anachronistic though it is, it is difficult not to visualise Somerset as a Shakespearean hero, flung from the heights as a result of some tragic flaw of character. He had everything; he finished with nothing. (However, his family was soon restored by the ever-generous Mary.) Almost all his friends and colleagues deserted him either in 1549 or in 1551: in 1549 Petre and Philip Hoby abandoned him, and Thomas Smith would have done the same if he could. Cecil played an ambiguous role, as did a number of others; even Thynne whined about the duke's love of building, and explained that he had often tried to dissuade him from such extravagance. At the time of the duke's second fall almost all his associates were concerned only to save their own skins: as one contemporary noted, when Somerset was executed, 'his councillors slept their collars turned their coats'. Such desertions were, of course, commonplace, and sixteenth-century political life would have been even bloodier without them, but it does seem that the duke was a man easily abandoned; Edward's cold comment in his journal that 'the Duke of Somerset had his head cut off upon Tower Hill between eight and nine o'clock in the morning' may, in fact, reveal as much about the duke as it does about the king.

Perhaps the duke's earlier abandonment of his brother, who did not even have, as Somerset did, the benefit of a trial, made his cause less attractive. Perhaps it was the fault of his wife. Anne Stanhope was described at the time of the duke's first fall as a woman of 'ambitious wit and mischievous persuasions, [who] led him and diverted him even also in the weighty affairs and governance of the realm'; this judgement was obviously widely shared, for in October 1549 it was reported by the Imperial ambassador that the duchess had been 'very badly handled in words by the courtiers and peasants, who put all this trouble down to her'. Certainly her pride and ambition produced tensions within the household, so that even Paget was willing to concede to van der Delft that Somerset had 'a bad wife'.

Perhaps, however, the fault was not all hers. Somerset was a man of many parts, some of them admirable, but others less so. As the anonymous French account suggests, he was a man of gracious speech and sometimes unkind action:

> de quelque entendement couvert et simulé en ces actions de la nature commune des Anglois/doux apparence gracieuses paroles at maligne volonté . . .

BIBLIOGRAPHICAL NOTE

I have not given footnote references to manuscripts which are inaccessible to the majority of students. (Most of those that I have used may be found in the Public Record Office, and the British Library.) Nor, for simplicity, have I given references when material is clearly taken from major printed sources. These, for Somerset's period of power, are the *Acts of the Privy Council of England*, ed. J. S. Dasent and others, 46 vols., (London, 1890-1964), vols I-IV; *Statutes of the Realm*, ed. A. Luders, T. E. Tomlins, J. Raithby and others (London, 1810-28); and *Tudor Royal Proclamations*, P. L. Hughes, and J. F. Larkin, eds., 3 vols., (New Haven, 1964-9). There is much of interest in the reports of foreign ambassadors, especially those of the Imperial ambassadors, in *Calendar of State Papers Spanish*, ed. G. A. Bergenroth and others (London, 1862-), volumes X and XI, and de Selve, Odet, *Correspondence politique*, ed. G. Lefèvre-Pontalis (Paris, 1888). Paget's letters are full of information: see, especially, *The Letters of William, Lord Paget of Beaudesert, 1547-63*, ed. B. L. Beer and S. M. Jack, *Camden Miscellany, XXV* (1974).

Secondary books that should be consulted include (in alphabetical order).

M. L. Bush, *The Government Policy of Protector Somerset* (London, 1975)

D. Hoak, *The King's Council in the Reign of Edward VI*, (Cambridge, 1976)

W. R. D. Jones, *The Tudor Commonwealth, 1529-1559* (London, 1970)

W. K. Jordan, *Edward VI: the Young King* (London, 1968) and *Edward VI: the Threshold of Power* (London, 1970)

W. K. Jordan, ed. *The Chronicle and Political Papers of King Edward VI*, (London, 1966)

J. N. King *English Reformation Literature. The Tudor Origins of the Protestant Tradition* (Princeton, 1982) 'Freedom of the Press, Protestant Propaganda, and Protector Somerset', *Huntington Library Quarterly*, XL (1976)

D. M. Loades, *The Reign of Edward VI* (Bangor, 1994).

'Protector Somerset, Patron of the English Renaissance', *Papers of the Bibliographical Society of America*, 70 (1976), 307-31

A. F. Pollard, *England under Protector Somerset: An Essay* (London, 1900)

W. Seymour, *Ordeal by Ambition: An English Family in the Shadow of the Tudors* (London, 1972)

D. Starkey, *The Reign of Henry VIII: Personalities and Politics* (London, 1985)

and, amongst articles:

G. Bernard,, The downfall of Sir Thomas Seymour', in *The Tudor Nobility*, ed. G. W. Bernard (Manchester, 1992)

G. R. Elton, 'Reform and the "Commonwealthmen" of Edward VI's Reign', in Clark, P., Smith, A. G. R. and Tyacke, N., eds. *The English Commonwealth, 1547-1640* (London, 1979)

A. J. A. Malkiewicz, 'An Eye-Witness's Account of the Coup d'Etat of October 1549', *English Historical Review*, 70 (1955), 600-9.